29.95

CREEP OUT

OLD JAILS

VALERIE BODDEN

CREATIVE ◖ EDUCATION

Published by Creative Education
P.O. Box 227, Mankato, Minnesota 56002
Creative Education is an imprint of The Creative Company
www.thecreativecompany.us

Design and production by Chelsey Luther
Art direction by Rita Marshall
Printed in China

Photographs by Alamy (Sandra Baker, catnap, Sinibomb Images, Atsuko Ellie Teramoto), Dreamstime (3dmentat, Butirano, Marcel Clemens, Dragoneye, Kyolshin, Lemonfluffy4upload, Glenn Nagel, Radiokafka, Sashkinw), Getty Images (De Agostini, OGphoto, Stacy Pearsall), iStockphoto (allanswart, Giorgio Fochesato)

Library of Congress Cataloging-in-Publication Data
Names: Bodden, Valerie, author.
Title: Old jails / Valerie Bodden.
Series: Creep out.
Includes bibliographical references and index.
Summary: Feel goosebumps begin to form as this title explores old jails around the world, surveying common jail and prison features and creepy stories about these places.

Identifiers: LCCN 2016033592 / ISBN 978-1-60818-809-3 (hardcover) / ISBN 978-1-56660-857-2 (eBook)
Subjects: LCSH: 1. Jails—Psychological aspects—Juvenile literature. 2. Haunted places—Juvenile literature. 3. Parapsychology—Juvenile literature.
Classification: LCC BF1461.B6345 2017 / DDC 133.1/22—dc23

CCSS: RI.1.1, 2, 3, 4, 5, 6, 10; RI.2.1, 2, 3, 4, 5, 6, 7, 10; RI.3.1, 2, 3, 4, 5, 10; RF.1.1, 3, 4; RF.2.3, 4; RF.3.3, 4

First Edition HC 9 8 7 6 5 4 3 2 1

Table *of* Contents

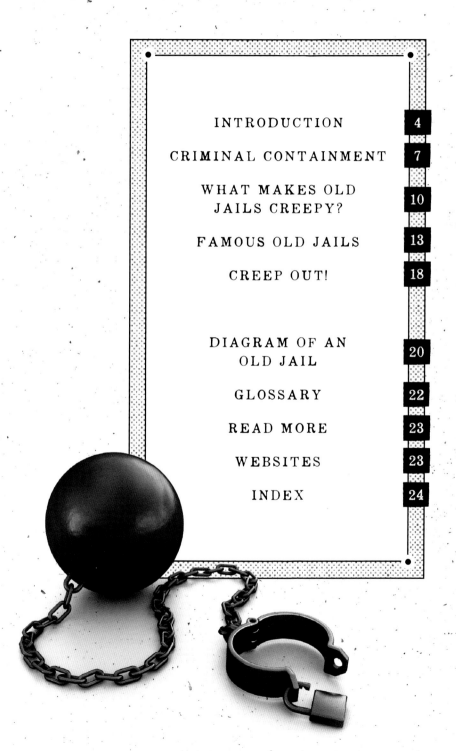

INTRODUCTION

YOUR footsteps echo. You strain to see down the dark corridor. Moist air clings to your skin. You shiver. You are in an old jail.

SOME OLD JAILS WERE MADE ON THE GROUND FLOOR (OR LOWER LEVELS) OF CASTLES.

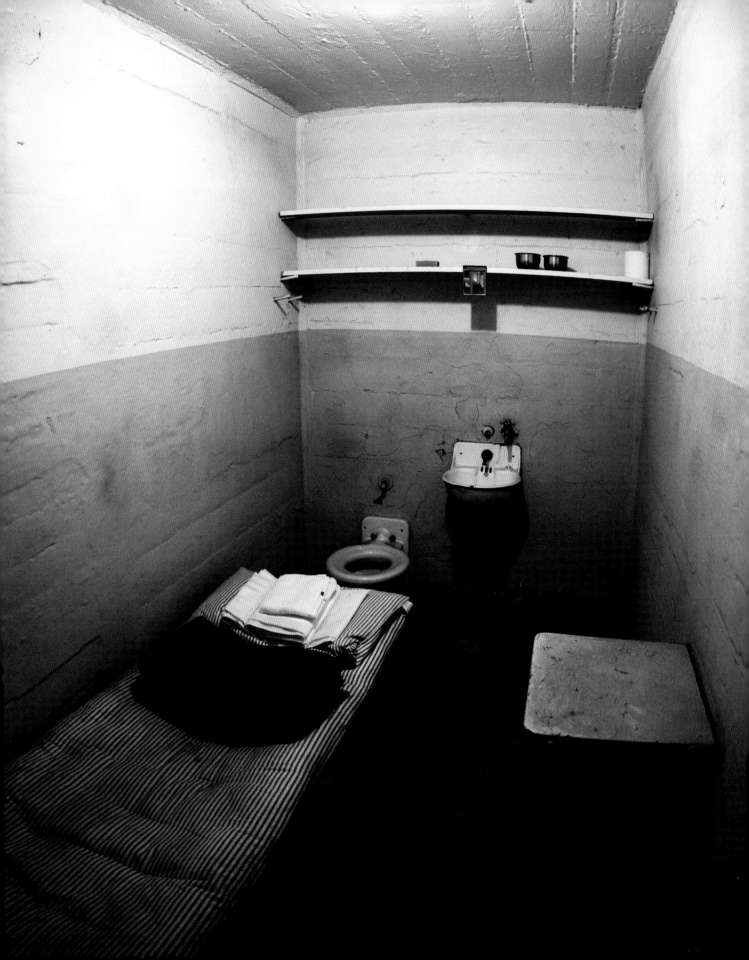

CRIMINAL CONTAINMENT

JAILS and prisons hold criminals. These people are locked in small rooms called cells. Some jails have space for a few criminals. Others can fit hundreds.

JAIL CELLS MIGHT HAVE A TOILET AND SINK BUT NO PIPES OR PARTS THAT COULD BE TORN OFF.

THE first prisons were built thousands of years ago. People in prisons were often treated badly. They might not be given much food or water. Sometimes they were tortured.

BEING CHAINED TO A WALL OR LOCKED IN A SPIKY BOX WERE POSSIBLE FORMS OF TORTURE.

What Makes Old Jails Creepy?

OLD prisons creep some people out. Paint flakes off crumbling walls. Bars on cells are worn and rusty. Empty cells might still hold prisoners' beds. Writing might cover cell walls, too. Some people think old prisons are haunted.

IMAGINING WHAT HAPPENED IN AN OLD JAIL CAN BE PART OF HOW CREEPY IT SEEMS.

Famous Old Jails

ALCATRAZ was built on an island in San Francisco Bay. It once held some of America's most dangerous criminals. They were not allowed to talk. Some tried to escape. But no one made it very far.

THREE MEN ESCAPED FROM ALCATRAZ IN 1962 AND WERE BELIEVED TO HAVE DROWNED IN THE BAY.

EASTERN State Penitentiary (*pen-ih-TEN-shuh-ree*) stands in Pennsylvania. It was used for 142 years. One famous prisoner was gangster Al Capone. He said he saw a ghost in the jail. Today, people think they hear footsteps and strange laughter.

IT IS THOUGHT THAT CAPONE'S SEVEN-MONTH STAY AT EASTERN STATE WAS FAIRLY COMFORTABLE.

THE Tower of London is a castle in England. It was built more than 900 years ago. Part of it was used as a prison. Many people were tortured and killed there. Some tourists say they've seen the prisoners' ghosts.

THE WHITE TOWER—THE LARGEST PART OF THE TOWER OF LONDON—WAS WHERE PRISONERS WERE KEPT.

TODAY, people can visit many old prisons. Are you brave enough to enter? Or will you get creeped out?

PEOPLE USED OLD JAILS LIKE EASTERN STATE AS MODELS FOR HOW TO BUILD NEWER PRISONS.

Diagram *of an* Old Jail

CELL DOOR

Only a few metal bars stood between guards and prisoners.

CELLS

Criminals spent long days here.

ENTRANCE

Some prisoners who went in never came out.

CORRIDOR

Once filled with the shouts of prisoners.

WINDOW

Small windows didn't let much light in. And they didn't let prisoners out.

Glossary

CORRIDOR—a long hall with rooms opening onto it

CRIMINALS—people who have broken the law

GANGSTER—a member of a group of criminals who commit crimes together

PENITENTIARY—a prison for people who committed serious crimes

TORTURED—purposely hurt as a form of punishment

TOURISTS—people who visit a place on a trip

Read More

Gordon, Nick. *Alcatraz*. Minneapolis: Bellwether Media, 2014.

Von Finn, Denny. *Tower of London*. Minneapolis: Bellwether Media, 2014.

Websites

Alcatraz Island

https://www.nps.gov/alca/index.htm
Find pictures and information about the island prison of Alcatraz.

Eastern State Penitentiary

http://www.easternstate.org/explore
Take an online tour of this old prison.

⚠ Note: Every effort has been made to ensure that any websites listed above were active at the time of publication and suitable for children. However, because of the nature of the Internet, it is impossible to guarantee that these sites will remain active indefinitely or that their contents will not be altered.

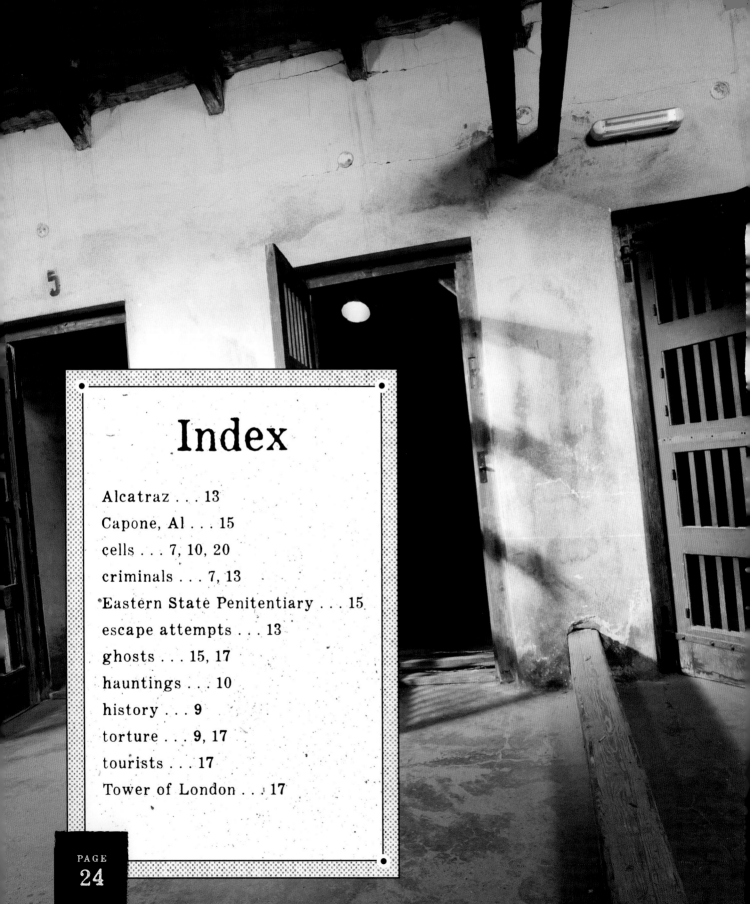

Index